# BLACK BOX 149

## R. JOHNS

CURRENCY PLAYS

First published in 2012
by Currency Press Pty Ltd,
PO Box 2287, Strawberry Hills, NSW, 2012, Australia
enquiries@currency.com.au
www.currency.com.au
in association with
La Mama Theatre, Melbourne.

This revised edition published 2012.

NATIONAL LIBRARY OF AUSTRALIA CIP DATA

| | |
|---|---|
| Author: | Johns, R. |
| Title: | Black box 149 / R Johns. |
| ISBN: | 9780868199436 (pbk.) |
| Dewey Number: | A822.4 |

Typeset by Dean Nottle for Currency Press. Cover design by Peter Mumford.
Front cover shows Dion Mills and Osamah Sami.

Currency Press acknowledges the Traditional Owners of the Country on which
we live and work. We pay our respects to all Aboriginal and Torres Strait
Islander Elders, past and present.

# Contents

*Black Box 149* was first produced at La Mama Theatre, Melbourne, on 15 September 2011 with the following cast:

| | |
|---|---|
| PILOT | Dennis Coard |
| MAN | Majid Shokor |

Director, Matt Scholten
Dramaturgical Adviser, Julian Meyrick
Set Design and Graphics, Peter Mumford
Lighting Design, Stelios Karagiannis
Stage Manager/Operator, Benjamin Morris
Audiovisuals, Brett Ludeman

## PLAYWRIGHT'S NOTE

The play is a fictionalised account based on a true incident.

August 2nd 1990, the day Kuwait was invaded, has become the day that started two Gulf Wars.

BA 149, the last commercial flight out of Kuwait Airport, was stranded as Saddam Hussein's forces invaded. The pilot, his crew and passengers were taken hostage and as 'guests' became human shields.

The story of that time is realised through the pilot's memory fragments as told to his daughter in a last will and testament. The pilot realises he was betrayed at a fundamental level—both then and now—by the duplicity of the West.

The black box is a metaphor for the pilot's mental landscape of confinement.

## ACKNOWLEDGEMENTS

To Liz Jones at La Mama for her long-time support of my work. The play had its first season at La Mama and was part of Melbourne Fringe Festival 2011.

To Julian Meyrick, who as dramaturgical adviser gave me invaluable and inspired insights into the structure and content of the play.

To Matt Scholten who directed the play. In a truly collaborative and joyous process Matt worked with me as writer and, together with the actors Dennis Coard and Majid Shokor, we made changes to the script as we went and created a very special show.

To Majid Shokor for generously sharing his story with me of life and times in Iraq, so I had a deep sense of the place and people. Majid has assisted with the translation of English into Arabic.

To the Open Eye program, Melbourne Fringe Festival, which provided me with Gary Abrahams as my mentor.

To Chris Bendall and theatre@risk Festival of New Writing where the play had a first reading in 2007, with Neil Pigot as the Pilot and Chris Bendall directing.

To Peter Mumford for our thorough discussions about the script, the Pilot and staging.

To Katrianne Abu Helewa who helped with my research and who was note-taker.

To all who gave generously of their time in the research including Efim Kishinevski, Michael Smith Warner, Antonio Piccolo and Graham Turner for discussions on code, guns, ballistics and being on the run.

To Peter Stratford for his acute ear for dialogue.

To Shahin Shafaei for his suggestions on camera and YouTube.

To Brian Williamson for the flight simulator experience.

To the crew: Peter Mumford who created the black box, Stelios Karagiannis who designed the lights, Benjamin Morris who ran the show at La Mama and Brett Ludeman who created our surreal film clip on the beach.

To all who have been a part of this project, their courage, honesty and commitment have been inspiring. Thank you.

## CHARACTERS

PILOT, 50 years of age. He is dedicated, very professional and proud of his profession. He has standards and always does his best to uphold them. His inability to do much as he discovers in surreal and bizarre circumstances how he has been betrayed, damages him. Yet he is heroic in the face of adversity. The impact of the trauma makes him feel alone and isolated.

MAN, plays multiple characters—the Hotel Manager, the Interrogator and the Bus Driver. He speaks Arabic. He is the mouthpiece for the Iraq/Kuwait experience, as remembered by the Pilot. As the Bus Driver he becomes the human face of Iraq's pain.

## SETTING

The setting is the mental landscape of the Pilot. He is trapped in a black box. Conceptually, this is his mind, therefore the black box is the interior mental landscape versus real space and time, which the actor can never leave or break out of. The black box also gives the history of BA flight 149 and the disputed facts. The black box serves as a metaphor for the claustrophobic imprisonment of the Pilot in Iraq, and in the rural hideout.

## LIGHTING

Enhances the feeling of entrapment, confusion and claustrophobia. Creates a sense of the cockpit, Iraq and the West. Also used to increase mystery and danger, where matches and candles become a single lighting source.

## COSTUME

• In the dual dialogue scene the Pilot and Man are dressed the same, both in singlets and dark trousers.
• Pilot only wears his full uniform at end of the play.
• Hotel manager in dishdasha, the ankle length robe and headgear ghotra and ogal.
• Interrogator dark trousers and jacket. Beret.

## STYLE

The style emphasises the atmosphere of fear, duplicity and entrapment. The body becomes a site of fear and terror.

Non-naturalism—with reference to Beckett—restriction. Non-naturalism in use of props. The boxes of matches used by the actors in the play become a metaphor for the shared stories between the characters. Matches illuminate the truth, matches are also thrown away, discarded, burnt. Matches are memories stored in a box. Matches become a universal language for cvs, photos, cigarettes, the list, names.

Shifting time lines, which merge in peculiar ways.

Transformation through physical gesture rather than costume, except where noted.

Transformation of an unchanging and restricted space through light and sound.

Telling a story in a language other than English is key to the play. Arabic can be found in the Appendix.

The layout and position of lines of dialogue give some indication of thought processes and rhythm.

The audience becomes like a Greek chorus, receiver of meaning.

## DESIGN

The design aesthetics are minimalist.

A black cube with a large hole cut in the fourth wall so the audience sees inside. The cube conveys a feeling of being trapped and relates to the Pilot hiding. There is a secret entrance in the back of the cube, which allows the Iraqi actor to appear and disappear into the blackness.

A video camera is hooked up. There are two chairs side by side, on the back of one hangs the Pilot's jacket. A dog trap and cutting/slashing implements—saw, shears, chain and barbed wire—hang suspended above the cube. The Pilot's feeling of being under threat is emphasised by these metallic implements hanging above his head like a sword of Damocles. Both actors are confined within the box—one hidden at times by a conceal within the structure of the box.

## LANGUAGE AND MUSIC

The Arabic, which is romanised, is as the Pilot remembers the sound of the language. The Arabic that is spoken as part of the Bus Driver's monologue is not romanised, as it is fluent and immediate. The Arabic/informal Iraqi text is written in the Appendix. As the writer, I have asked the actor from the first production, Majid Shokor, who grew up in Iraq, and who is a recent immigrant to Australia after the First Gulf War, to be the translator. He is a classically trained actor and calligrapher. I have followed his advice as to how to set out the Bus Driver's monologue in the Appendix. He has translated it into both the formal (literal) form and the informal (street parlance) form. In the street parlance much of the poetry is gone, but I want the reader to have the experience of both.

In production we also added more Arabic/informal Iraqi to both Interrogator scenes, particularly the first one. The Interrogator plays with the Pilot—deliberately confuses him, to throw him off balance, e.g., the rules of the matchbox game are explained in part in Arabic. This is very much worked between the two actors on the floor.

In the first production the Iraqi actor Majid Shokor sang, in the second production the Iraqi actor Osamah Sami played the oud. The oud is an ancient Middle Eastern stringed instrument, a great, great, great ancestor to the guitar. The oud has a haunting, melancholic sound. It is said to have the power to affect the emotions and sensibility of the listener. The actor explored how best to use the oud with the text. The wonderfulness of discovery helped the work continue to evolve. The oud in the production was played three times, always in connection to particular references to Amy; first Amy/Hassan, then Amy's bedtime story of the minotaur and the later retelling of that story in Babylon.

The script is very flexible regarding the skill sets of the actors. The co-pilot in the second production was played with a South African accent, with Afrikaans words thrown in (e.g., kleintjie (tiny) as description of the dog and braai vleis (roast meat), etc.). The co-pilot Dion Mills played came from Johannesburg. Dennis Coard's co-pilot came from Belfast.

*PRE-SET: The box of the set is isolated by a soft pool of light all around it. The box itself (3 metres x 3 metres) is not lit. There are dangerous agricultural and avionic (wiring) implements hanging directly above the box. Cross fade. Lights around the box go to black. Lights in box come up. Two chairs as in a cockpit set up, one has a Pilot's jacket draped over it, the other a Pilot's shirt.*

*SCENE ONE*

PILOT: [*to the camera*] I am being watched. Through the crosshair of a rifle. The eye pressed to the glass. Waiting. For the moment. To pull the trigger. I am being watched from far away. No mail in months. Then the farmer's boy comes up here with a package. It's been opened and resealed. Inside the photo…

You… Amy. You're with a man. Blurred shot outside a cafe. Scrawled on the back.

Dad… I want you to know… I've met someone. His name is Hassan.

> *He withdraws from the camera.*

The farmer's son is seven.
He didn't open the package. He just wants five bucks for the delivery.

[*As the* FARMER'S SON] Please mister. It's my pocket money.

Skips back down the hill… throws stones at the perimeter fence. A wild dog nailed there. Freshly killed. Not flayed.

Yes I am being warned.

Sky turns yellow. A dust storm is coming. It's hard to shoot accurately in a hot northerly. Best of luck, you bastards. Get me if you can.

Amy. Lovely Amy. I want you to know that you are… It's you I think of each morning… but this alarms me. Who is this… man? How did you meet him? In a library? A bus stop? Did he sit next to you? Across from you? Staring at you? Did he follow you day after day?

Was he the first one to strike up a conversation?

[*As* HASSAN] Excuse me, I am stranger here. How do I get to—?

Forgive me… may I ask your name? Let me introduce myself. My name is Hassan. You are very pretty. May I ask your father's permission to go out with you…? Where does your father live…? What does he do?

[*To the camera*] My dad is a loser. A drifter. That is what you must say. He does not belong in my life anymore.

You are not to tell him anything about me. I do not exist. I am blank. Zero. Cipher. *Sifr*… empty like the desert.

I am not helpless like then.

Stop this now.

Break it up.

Tell her. It is impossible.

This man will kill you. Or me.

That's it. Explain rationally. Why he is not good for her.

When she knows the story.

The true story of what happened in the desert. She won't want him anymore.

Go on.

You're not paralysed like before. You're free to speak…

[*Looking out to void space*] … till they come to get me.

[*To the camera*] Amy love. I didn't just walk away. That's what your mother said.

[*Withdraws from camera*] No, she'll say same old, same old.

This man you've met. Is he from…?

Is he an Arab?

I don't understand the Arab mind.

They turn in a moment, from being friendly to wanting to cut your throat. Full of revenge. Don't think anything through.

[*As* AMY] Oh, Dad, you are such a racist.

Never!

Is he Iraqi? Because he could be.

Amy, as you walk in the rain or get on a bus. You cannot escape terror. The man, Hassan, who sits next to you, what's his history? What terror is he carrying in his briefcase, his backpack, and his heart? But he's not alone. What eyes are watching you? Because the woman with the packages on her knee, the man in the city suit, the bus driver are all contaminated by terror.

There was a war.

Before 9/11… Which—have an open mind—was not ground zero. The Americans forget… they created ground zero with the atomic bomb; the Manhattan Project and Hiroshima.

I don't want you to be stupid, Amy.

Life isn't all Facebook and amnesia about the history of the real world.

That won't go down well…

A war… in this war the terror came from the air.

Do you even remember its name?

I got caught up in that.

Why give a fuck? Care factor zero.

It's why they are watching me now. Every last memory has to be wiped out. So it becomes a silent history.

Only the lies live on. How will she know?

Tape's an obsolete technology, as obsolete as truth-telling. Who would bother playing them back?

If today I tell you this… it's because you must understand why this man will be no good for you.

You need someone who is loyal, who you can trust and who will not betray you.

[*As* AMY] Look in the mirror, Dad. Wake up to yourself.

You see your father as a loser because he never came back? Do you ever stop to think, sweetheart, why this happened?

Once I held a job.

*Sound effects of aircraft taking off.*

Bravo Alpha 149. A flick of turbulence. Brace yourself... this is your flight. We are cruising at an altitude of 35,000 feet. There's a dust storm coming up. Great yellow clouds swirling violently over Basra. If you look down to your left the land is brown. Covered in dust. Clear the dials of dust. This is my plane.

Who am I?

A pilot.

Am I?

A pilot.

Go on then. Show me.

My job—was to fly planes high up.

How could I be so hopeless they said and get stuck on the ground?

[*British accent of authority*] You need to realise that's why we can't keep you on...

Until that day in the desert I was fearless.

Once upon a time your father saw himself as invincible. Indestructible.

This is not a point of view. It's a confession.

The story you know, Amy, is not this story. You won't recognise it.

The desert. Where the terror came. A place so removed from any understandable reality. Where everything was lost.

The knot in the guts.

It was the same when your mum left.

Everything became broken.

Just because she took you didn't mean I wasn't going to be there for you.

I made you. We made you.

You're so precious to me.

But when people are angry at each other…

I just had to handle the situation with kid gloves.

*He stares at his hands.*

Gloves.

Gloves? For a pilot! [*Looking at the camera*] Your mother always wanted me to be something else. Something trapped on the ground. In a safe job. Home at five. Tea on the table. A cosy, safe life.

[*Withdraws from camera*] She never understood.

Hands have to feel the controls, the brutality of the machine.

How do you fly a commercial airline? By navigation. By technology. What causes most planes to crash? Metal fatigue, systems failure or pilot error.

I didn't know she was going to walk out.

How can you control something when you don't know what is happening?

I always wanted the best for you.

*Pause.*

I did.

When you were eight years' old. How you cried when we said you couldn't have a dog because you had asthma.

I want something to love you said. I have nothing to love.

I don't know when it died. The love. The feelings between your mother and me.

She'd get obsessively jealous about all the stewardesses. Blonde, pretty, want to marry a pilot. She made it all up in her head.

She'd watch us walk out of the airport terminal, pulling our smart little trolley bags behind us.

[*As the* PILOT'S WIFE] Who's she? The one with the red lips.

Emma…

Emma left red lipstick on cigarettes and glasses.

She'd laugh; the Arab women don't paint their mouths. Their mouths are silent. Not mine…

Silence. Your mother's endless silences. Days of them. I didn't know what I'd done.

Like being a kid again. The silence.

Dad, home from the Second World War… stopped speaking. Amazing I got born really. Took twenty years. A drunken night.

What did Dad do in the war, Mum?

[*As the* PILOT'S MUM] He was a desert rat at Tobruk.

As a kid I'd sit at the table watching this silent man at the table refuse to talk.

All I ever gleaned from Mum was that the Stukas terrified him. The screaming German aeroplanes.

These special bars flapped down from the wings—as the plane went into a dive—and the wind rushing past the grid made a shrieking sound.

He was terrified to look up in the skies and see these devilish winged creatures, Mum'd say, but sssh! [*Quietly*] Don't talk about it. Shameful. He can't keep a job down. Breakdown after breakdown. He's not quite right in the head.

Running away to the pub.

Boom! Massive heart attack at fifty.

I was still a kid. I vowed: I'm not going that way.

It's why I became a pilot. I was fearless. I would be the one in the sky, not the terrified creature trembling on the earth.

Women want to keep you on the earth.

Not Emma… Emma.

I don't know what happened to her.

It gets uncomfortable. When a woman fancies you and you don't re-ciprocate. They sort of disappear.

Or you disappear.

    *Pause.*

Your mother always said I had a limited imagination.

[*With a laugh*] Shallow, was her favourite word. Shallow as that tube in the sky you fly in.

The knot in my guts.

[*To the camera*] You have to understand the truth. I never wanted you to feel you had to take sides. It's why I let things slide. And you don't want to upset your mum, contacting me. [*To void space*] But I never had an affair with Emma.

Your mother dreamt that up. I never wanted to cause you pain.

The day she walked out with you, Amy. I washed the dishes very care-fully, looking out the window. Rinsed and rinsed.

[*As* AMY] Goodbye, Dad.

I kept my back turned. Washing the dishes. Not to look at your face.

[*As the* PILOT'S WIFE] Get in the car. If he wants to say goodbye he can wave from the window. He can see the driveway from the window.

Rinse. Stack. Wipe. Rinse. Stack. How can I live day in day out like this?

What's the point? It's what we became. All of us. Collateral damage.

Our pain.

Their pain.

    *Silence.*

What do you think she's going to feel when she learns her father has been found dead?

How will she live with that?

Windows and doors locked.

[*Looking at the camera*] Paranoia is not a family trait, Amy.

They will tell you I am mad, deranged, or clinically depressed. The pharmaceutical evidence will be cited, prescription drugs, sleeping pills, anti-depressants. Bathroom cabinet full. Emptied bottles.

I'm on the list to be hunted down. Take your pick to my likely cause of death.

Whatever leaves no trace behind… those bastards out there will search this place.

They might prop me up in this chair, but I can't have rope marks on my wrists to show I was tied. It may no longer look like suicide as they put the rifle between my legs, jam it in my mouth and pull the trigger. *Boom!*

But when it is taken care of.

The death notice will be placed discreetly. He was a valuable employee but had been stood down, paid out. Unable to cope. Will be greatly missed.

Read the death notices.

To hell with conspiracy theories I moved lock, stock and barrel, left what happened far behind. But then the letters start arriving.

Letter one. What happened on the other side of the world twenty years ago will ruin your life.

No-one will escape. Unsigned.

Letter two. Watch your back. All knowledge will be eliminated. X. I tear it up. I've been quiet. Letter three. Why did you do what you did? Who helped you survive? Remember you can be detained and no-one will ever know. Dog.

Why?

I'm not rewriting history. That's their game. The victors write their official version of events.

[*To the camera*] But go to WikiLeaks, Amy. Proof. Last words.Out of the limelight the US Ambassador April Glaspie meets with Saddam Hussein post the Iran-Iraq War, 1990.

[*American accent*] We Americans have no opinion on your Arab-Arab conflicts, like your border disagreement with Kuwait.

So what happens when Saddam goes ahead with his plans?

[*To void space.*] August 2nd 1990. British Airways flight 149. Outbound Heathrow to Kuwait. Kuwait to Kuala Lumpur.

I am in a hotel in Kuwait, just flown in from Malaysia, and will take Flight 149 to KL. I am fast asleep in the hotel, when someone bangs on my door and shoves a note under it.

Flight 149 delayed in Heathrow two hours. The auxiliary unit in the tail of the plane defective, requires repair to control air-conditioning. You now need to report to Kuwait Airport terminal four a.m.

Innocuous then.

But now as I look back, what else is in the tail of the plane?

The black box. The oracle. The truth-seeker. The truth-speaker.

So is the auxiliary unit being repaired or the is black box being removed?

Why would a black box be removed?

If there was to be no record of flight 149.

Every time I fly, I live with death. The plane could crash. When people fly there is always a chance they could die, it goes with the territory.

But do people imagine the government sees their lives as worthless? That passengers and crew on a western commercial flight could be brutalised and murdered? I believe that's what Bush Senior and Thatcher hoped for. Saddam's henchmen would disappear us in the shifting sands.

Margaret Thatcher stood in front of the House of Commons. [*As* THATCHER] We would *never* allow a civilian flight to land or take off in a war zone. *The invasion was later*.

Would anyone really believe the British Government would ever be investigated for the great lies, in their unchallenged version of what really happened that day?

Who am I?

A pilot.

A pilot who is a threat to national security.

The game works this way: Isolate yourself. Talk to no-one. Deny everything. Those days press delete.

*He smells the sleeve of his jacket.*

The Australian smell. Beer. The Arab smell. Sweat.

Gives me a knot in my guts.

*The* MAN *enters and very quietly sings in Arabic, a counterpoint to the* PILOT*'s words. He chalks in large Arabic script 'down with the dictator' on the wall behind the* PILOT.

[*Whispering*] Don't lose it. Keep it together. Too easy to lose it.

When I think of you, Amy, I'm reading you bedtime stories.

Otherwise you'd burrow under the bedclothes with your torch

You'll ruin your eyes.

[*As* AMY] But Mum says it's time for lights out and I want to be a princess. Ariadne, hand in hand with the prince, and kill the monster. Half bull. Half man. He eats human flesh. Hidden in the labyrinth. He's scary. Who kills the Minotaur? Read it, Dad.

Ariadne gives the prince a thread at the entrance to the labyrinth so he can find his way out. He tells her he loves her.

[*As* AMY] Do you love me, Dad?

That's a silly question.

[*As* AMY] Do you?

But then the prince abandons Ariadne.

[*As* AMY] Does she cry?

He wants her dead.

[*As* AMY] Would you ever want me dead?

Never.

I never wanted anyone to hurt you.

> *The* MAN *exits.*

This is the proof. I am ready now.

*SCENE TWO*

*The* PILOT *now more as the alpha male, stronger. He puts on the pilot's shirt.*

PILOT: Four in the morning. Kuwait Airport.

> Sleepy.

Terminal quiet.

Crews cross over.

Here I am taking over the flight.

Sitting in the cockpit—calling the tower.

Waiting to fly into the darkness.

The throb of the engines beneath me.

This is Bravo Alpha 149 to Kuwait Tower. Over… Bravo Alpha 149 Tower, are you receiving me?

> *Pause.*

Also in the cockpit. George Bryant. Union all the way, from Belfast. He hates the bosses. He's my co-pilot.

> *Retaining the accuracy of the experience, he speaks with* GEORGE'*s accent.*

[*As* GEORGE] Fuck! We're stuck here. It looks like they are closing the airport.

> *Change of tone.*

Why?

[*As* GEORGE] Don't know, mate.

Get some clarification from the control tower.

> *Sound effects of white noise.*

The tower still isn't responding.

[*As* GEORGE] Kuwait, mate… could be a VIP route… anything.

He yells at the steward. [*As* GEORGE] Justin, time to spray your hair, darlin', looks like they've just closed the airport. Stewardess! Ah, Emma love! Make us a coffee, will you?

Grates on my nerves. Sitting there waiting to go.

Now it's dawn. Trails of light across the sky. The sun glinting on the wings.

There's this…

*B… boom!*

[*As* GEORGE] What the fuck was that?

[*Turning and looking*] Flies right past, a fighter dropping these flare decoys out the back.

*B… boom…* Another one.

[*As* GEORGE] Third World crackpots! Kuwait Air Force… are they fucking blind? They're just chucking those things out the back. Is this a military parade? Oh, what! They're fucking bomb carriers.

Justin pale as a ghost, safety checks complete. [*As* JUSTIN] Are we clear to take off? What's the control tower say?

Same message. Closed.

I'm sitting there. Looking out the cockpit window. Then suddenly.

Snap. We've got to evacuate the aircraft.

*Boom!*

[*As* JUSTIN] Everyone's half asleep. It's six in the morning. How can we get them all off the aircraft?

[*As* GEORGE] Hang on, mate.

I can't be responsible. Anything could happen. I don't have clearance for take-off. We could be blown to bits just sitting here.

[*As* GEORGE] Fuck! That was an explosion.

Get the people off the aircraft. Now.

This is your captain. This is your captain. This is an emergency. Leave your hand baggage. Evacuate the aircraft immediately. I repeat. Evacuate the aircraft immediately.

And we're running into the terminal.

Passengers dazed.

Airport flight information boards.

All flights cancelled.

The knot. In the guts.

[*To the camera*] How is it on this day, British Airways is the only Western airline in the world that doesn't realise something is amiss?

There's a phone in the terminal. I get through to London.

What is going on?

Black smoke on the runway.

Explosions of sand. Artillery exchange.

And there's this great tank rolling over fleeing Kuwaitis and this bloke with a sort of Soviet-type helmet with an automatic rifle. Shooting wildly.

[*To the camera*] British Airways don't know. [*To void space*] They don't know anything about anything.

[*British accent*] Maybe it's a national holiday.

This airport has huge glass windows.

The sun is rising on fire.

Fire. Blazing outside.

[*As* GEORGE] I am fucking furious. This is all fucking wrong. We're sitting ducks here. I used to date a bird with big tits at ITV. We'll tell the fucking media.

I watch the crew.

Calming passengers. Selfless. Dedicated.

[*As* JUSTIN] Quiet. Quiet! Everything is under control. We are receiving instructions from London.

I get through to Independent Television Network.

We're a BA flight. All the passengers have been evacuated off the plane in Kuwait.

We've currently been delayed but at least we are all well.

Phone goes dead.

[*As* GEORGE] You fucking idiot, how could you downplay it like that? Dial them back!

No. Wait and see. Someone will do something helpful. This is British Airways.

Sure enough, five minutes later.

[*British accent*] British Airways here. What's being said by the crew to the press? *On no account* talk to television networks.

I'm trying to find out what's going on...

[*British accent*] This is a serious breach of your employment contract. You are not authorised to offer comment to the media about events, incidents or any other matter relating to the company, its employees or customers. We will have a moral and legal obligation to institute strong disciplinary action against you. You are not there to talk about what is going on.

[*To the camera*] But what is going on?

And then abruptly the line goes dead.

[*To void space*] We have to do something. Before panic sets in, we exit the terminal... get to the safety of the adjacent airport transit hotel.

The hotel manager Mr Hamad greets us.

HOTEL MANAGER: *Allah u Akbar*. God is great! Jesus too!

You have just, *Al'humdillilah*, missed the great Iraqi army over-whelming the small Kuwait forces in Terminal Two.

PILOT: Is this a war?

HOTEL MANAGER: I know British. I know Iraqis. [*Tapping his heart*] I am a good go-between.

PILOT: A go-between is what we have in the West when the nuclear family breaks down.

When I use my daughter to talk to my wife, because she's not talking to me.

So we sit at the dinner table and all the conversation is channelled through the child.

Tell your mother to pass the bread.

Tell your father I won't be here much longer. Can't stand it anymore.

HOTEL MANAGER: We don't always talk to our wives if they are angry, that is a Western affectation.

PILOT: Good advice on how to solve marital difficulties. But as to the more pressing matter, what is going on?

HOTEL MANAGER: You wait. The Iraqi army representative will come. You wait.

PILOT: So we wait and wait and wait in this hotel surrounded by tanks in blistering heat.

We watch soldiers blow up some of the runways, then men in blue overalls start digging trenches.

HOTEL MANAGER: May God protect you. If Saddam wills it, they cut your throats in the trenches.

PILOT: It's not possible. This has got to finish tomorrow or the next day.

HOTEL MANAGER: Finish, yes. Saddam says where there is person there is problem, no person, no problem. He will bury you alive. May God favour you.

PILOT: How about you let us use your phone to call the British Embassy?

HOTEL MANAGER: Very dangerous. Do not talk for long. We are all being watched.

PILOT: I dial the British Consul. His wife answers.

[*As the* CONSUL'S WIFE] My husband is out.

We are prisoners here.

[*As the* CONSUL'S WIFE] He will return your call.

Click. Call after call. Day in, day out. Always the same response.

[*As the* CONSUL'S WIFE] My husband is out.

Our situation is desperate.

[*As the* CONSUL'S WIFE] Yes. Goodbye.

What is going on? The same bizarre dead end.
Gut ache.

Mr Hamad is right. We are watched closely. The Iraqis are looking for weakness.

Have to show the Iraqis. Be normal. What's the best way to be…?

I break my rule. I look into Emma's eyes.

She stands close. I can feel the heat of her body through her silk shirt. Her mouth looks like a rosebud.

[*As* EMMA] People want someone to be in charge.

*He puts on a jacket and paces back and forth.*

I parade every day in fifty-centigrade heat with full uniform on. Do not take jacket off.

Observe! To report anything to the British Government—when we get back.

Since they are obviously in the dark about the events taking place.

Blast of hot wind. Sand in eyes.

Sweat. Dripping off my back, under my armpits.

Soaking into my shirt. [*To the camera*] Shirt clings to my skin like slime.

Handwash shirt before sleep. Hang it up to dry.

For morning show in full uniform.

> *He picks up a matchbox and stares at it. With this comes the memory.*

> *The* INTERROGATOR *enters behind him, with a matchbox, and strikes a match. He watches the flame burn out. He is really focused on the* PILOT. *The* PILOT *resists the urge to look at him. The* INTERROGATOR *lights matches and throws them away.*

INTERROGATOR: *Shlnak? Inta thib chiy law tamir?*

PILOT: I don't understand.

INTERROGATOR: *Inta amlk zane?*

PILOT: What is happening?

INTERROGATOR: You are a guest.

PILOT: Then I need help.

INTERROGATOR: What kind of help? *What do you want?*

PILOT: [*an echo*] *What do you want?*

> *The echo indicates the* PILOT*'s memory of what the* INTERROGATOR *said. Voices in unison are italicised. See Appendix for Arabic/ Iraqi spoken by Interrogator.*

I need to listen to the radio. To the BBC. I believe my wife and child might be in a studio. Sending best wishes.

INTERROGATOR: [*throwing his matchbox between his hands*] We have our people listening to the radio. Let's play a game. We flip a box of matches.

PILOT: Why?

INTERROGATOR: Time to give you a cultural lesson about Iraq. We play this game. Flip it… see… I am king. If the matchbox in this position, I am King here… you will do whatever I say. If you flip it right way… you are the guest… I do whatever you say.

PILOT: Best of three.

INTERROGATOR: [*tossing the matchbox again between his hands*] Again. I am king.

PILOT: Just one more chance.

INTERROGATOR: No Iraq way. Now tell me [*shaking the matchbox*] what happened to the twelve followers of Jesus Christ?

PILOT: What?

INTERROGATOR: What? You know nothing of the Special Forces on your plane?

PILOT: I am a pilot. I know nothing of the passengers.

INTERROGATOR: What passengers! On a military airplane?

PILOT: This was a commercial flight.

INTERROGATOR: Camouflaged by painting the plane.

PILOT: British Airways don't carry Special Forces on their planes.

INTERROGATOR: Who were these people and why did you land here?

    *The* INTERROGATOR *strikes a match.*

PILOT: The plane landed in Kuwait to refuel. We were the transit crew and took over.

INTERROGATOR: Where did the plane come from?

PILOT: London.

INTERROGATOR: Tell me about the twelve men. What their mission is. Then I promise you will leave here safely.

PILOT: I have no idea what you are talking about.

INTERROGATOR: What is your rank in the army? Are you in the army?

PILOT: No.

INTERROGATOR: You are responsible for the men under your command.

PILOT: I am not in the army. Who are you?

INTERROGATOR: [*with a laugh*] I am your friend. Tell me how many on your plane?

PILOT: Close to four hundred.

INTERROGATOR: How many are soldiers?

PILOT: I don't know.

INTERROGATOR: What else did you bring from London?

PILOT: I didn't come from London. I was the transit crew in Kuwait.

INTERROGATOR: Because you are part of intelligence?

PILOT: No. This is how BA operates.

INTERROGATOR: Why is an Australian working for BA?

PILOT: My wife is British.

INTERROGATOR: The first crew who left the plane, what happened to them?

PILOT: I don't know.

> The INTERROGATOR *moves in front of the* PILOT, *crossing between*
> *him and the empty chair.*

INTERROGATOR: That pilot has fled with some of his crew. He is underground somewhere. Why did that plane come to Kuwait? Did you not
hear on your BBC of the Iraq liberation of Kuwait? Did the American
spy satellites not tell you? Why were you not contacted by the au-
thorities to divert the plane?

PILOT: I knew nothing.

> The INTERROGATOR *lights another match and holds it up.*

INTERROGATOR: *Take a look at these photos. Is that your plane?*

PILOT: [*an echo*] *Take a look at these photos. Is that your plane?*

INTERROGATOR: What is being unloaded?

PILOT: Steel boxes.

INTERROGATOR: What are they?

PILOT: Don't know.

INTERROGATOR: Not food. Quite different shapes and sizes. What are they?

PILOT: You tell me.

INTERROGATOR: You are lying. If you keep doing this, *you will not see*
*the light of the sun again.*

PILOT: [*an echo*] *You will not see the light of the sun again.*

INTERROGATOR: Be good guy. Nice boy and tell the truth.

PILOT: I didn't fly the plane from London. I am transit crew. I came from
Malaysia to Kuwait.

INTERROGATOR: You keep telling lies, Australian. Another document. Look at this. [*He strikes a match.*] Your CV. You were a military pilot before.

PILOT: Never.

INTERROGATOR: You took part in the Falklands War. Bombed Argentineans.

PILOT: No. I have always been a commercial pilot. My wife would never have married a military pilot.

INTERROGATOR: Why?

PILOT: Too dangerous.

INTERROGATOR: So all military pilots in Britain and Australia have no wives?

PILOT: My wife is not happy I am a commercial pilot.

INTERROGATOR: You are a military pilot. These boxes. We have in store. We know what is in there. Military weapons. Tracking devices. Rocket launchers.

PILOT: Impossible.

INTERROGATOR: I can take you there and you can have a look. See our soldiers posing there

PILOT: You planted all this stuff. Propaganda.

INTERROGATOR: You create this conspiracy and bring everyone here.

PILOT: I did not come from London.

INTERROGATOR: [*lighting a match*] Do you like movies? What is your favourite film? *Gandhi?* No? *Lawrence of Arabia?* [*He blows out the match.*] Have you seen *Lawrence of Arabia*?

PILOT: Yes.

INTERROGATOR: I have seen many times in London. I finish my education there. Military course.

PILOT: How long?

INTERROGATOR: Two years.

PILOT: So you made friends there. You understand British ways.

INTERROGATOR: To some extent.

PILOT: This isn't fair play.

INTERROGATOR: A military pilot talking about fair play? You were honoured after the Falklands War. We find your name in the documents.

PILOT: A coincidence. I have spent my life as a commercial pilot. I have a family.

INTERROGATOR: What about the people you bombed in the Falklands. Don't they have families? How do you feel about Saddam liberating Kuwait?

PILOT: I have no opinion.

INTERROGATOR: You land undercover operatives to spy on our installations, our troop movements.

PILOT: Why are we being detained?

INTERROGATOR: Saddam will unite the Arab world. Iraqi land was taken by the British and given to thugs to create Kuwait. You are a military pilot. I have no doubt.

PILOT: Have the embassies been informed we are now detained as prisoners?

INTERROGATOR: Your embassy asked for the twelve SAS to join the Kuwaiti resistance. Your head of embassy works for spy service. You telephone him. Why?

PILOT: For help, but he's never there. This war has nothing to do with the crew, my passengers or me. We need, at the very least, hand baggage and medical supplies. Everything we need is still on the plane.

INTERROGATOR: Be grateful. We are not animals ready to cut your throat. You talk of fair play, pilot. Why does the world insist Iraq get out of Kuwait? But no-one insists Israel get out of Palestine. Israelis are illegal occupiers. But, pilot, I know all about fair play…

*The* INTERROGATOR *exits.*

PILOT: So there are George and I with an escort of armed soldiers.

[*As* GEORGE] For fuck's sake, whose stupid idea was this? Pick up four hundred pieces of fucking hand luggage!

Duck. Run. Weave. Cross the airfield past the last remnants of Kuwaiti resistance. Barrage of fire and missiles. And there she is. BA plane flight 149, still standing.

Soldiers weighed down with eau de Cologne, toothpaste, aftershave and socks.

Like the Christmas presents your mother would buy. I don't know what your father wants. Get him socks. You can never go wrong with socks.

George is thirsty. [*As* GEORGE] Bugger this. I need a scotch. The whiskey is in the hold. Who's the officer in charge? Listen, sunshine, open the hold. Him and me are in need of liquid refreshment.

We're in the hold.

[*As* GEORGE] Who's the fucking idiot barking like a dog?

Shit a brick, in the crate, there's a fucking wee dog.

*He bends down as if picking up the dog.*

It's yelping for joy.

[*As* GEORGE] Go on, lick the captain. *Aww!* Look at his name tag! Biggles! Biggles, you fucking hero, you have survived in temperatures well in excess of fifty degrees centigrade. You could have been roast meat, Biggles. Like your poor friend here.

Smell of dead dog in crate next to Biggles.

A big dog. Tongue hanging out. Purple.

George holds that little scrap of life.

Wriggling. Panting.

Sheer joy.

[*As* GEORGE] Bugger the scotch. Do you see? It's a sign. All creatures great and small. Jesus is on our side.

What, this animal's made you a Christian, has it?

[*As* GEORGE] I'm a Christian now, comrade, and so is Biggles. No-one will dare crucify us now.

We march back to the terminal. George carries Biggles.

What did the Iraqi bloke want from you, he asks?

I take the dog off George.

Hold it tight.

Black hole.

Falling through a black hole.

> *The* INTERROGATOR *enters and strikes a match.*

INTERROGATOR: You want to stay here because your wife wants to divorce you. You are angry. You don't want to go back to the West. You can marry an Iraqi. I can arrange a meeting. You don't have to leave. But you will have to serve in Iraqi forces. I am giving you a job and a wife. What more do you need? I wouldn't hesitate to be in London if you could provide me a wife and an opportunity in British Air Force.

You have a child. How old is she?

PILOT: Eight years' old. I have to go back for her. Do you have children?

INTERROGATOR: What do you think?

PILOT: If you had children you'd understand.

INTERROGATOR: Don't tell me you are concerned with children. All you are concerned about is oil and power. Let me make things easy for you. All the evidence is here. Photos we took.

> *The* INTERROGATOR *lights a match. He holds it so the* PILOT *is looking into the flame.*

This photo. Who is this child? Eight years' old. Blonde piggytails, blue eyes. In purple school uniform. Who is she? Is that your house? Nice house! She is just leaving the house?

PILOT: You are lying. What do you care about a little girl?

INTERROGATOR: We have connections. Cultural attachés all over the Western world and in your country. We have sympathisers and informers. So easy we can reach her.

PILOT: What do you want from me?

INTERROGATOR: Tell the truth.

PILOT: I am.

INTERROGATOR: I am showing you the evidence we have.

PILOT: I would tell you anything to save my child. Do you think I would sacrifice my daughter?

I don't know what the British Government is doing. I don't understand.

INTERROGATOR: [*clapping*] Bravo. You amuse me, pilot. Let us see who now wins the game. Flip the box… [*He flips the box.*] See, now you are king… what do you want?

PILOT: A shower.

INTERROGATOR: So small thinking! Do you want to go?

PILOT: Go where?

INTERROGATOR: Leave… [*He snaps his fingers.*] Like this.

PILOT: What?

INTERROGATOR: Leave. Get passengers and go.

PILOT: Of course.

INTERROGATOR: Where do you want aircraft to go? My soldiers will make Iraqi Airways team to be at your disposal, captain.

PILOT: Why?

INTERROGATOR: You think Saddam is dangerous. You are even more dangerous in your complacency. You stroll in your parks; you drink your coffee and your beer and congratulate yourself on your open mindedness. You do not know that a breath away is death.

PILOT: I will need to check the aircraft first.

INTERROGATOR: When streets are filled with the dead and cities reduced to rubble just remember we can reach your daughter at any moment. When she is eight, or eighteen, or even twenty-eight. Who knows what we will do to her? She will be an honour killing for the war orphans of Iraq. [*Casually*] *Your daughter will never be safe.*

PILOT: [*an echo*] *Your daughter will never be safe.*

Fuck you, you bastard.

Fuck you!

Get out of this hellhole.

Escape the madness.

I wake up everybody in the hotel.

[*Announcement*] We are leaving on BA flight 149, seven o' clock this morning. The crew will check out the aircraft then you can board.

The plane's been sitting there for weeks... fifty-five degrees centigrade...

That's the air temperature outside.

Inside the aircraft.

Blistering heat.

Burning hot.

And the stench!

A fully catered aircraft for four hundred people...

All this food on the air bridges

And it's sloshing out like soup...

Horrible

Rotting

Stuff...

In the cockpit I'm vomiting.

Justin has his plastic gloves on.

[*As* JUSTIN, *holding his hands up*] I don't care how many sick bags we fill. I don't care if everyone throws up as they get on the aeroplane. I just want to click my little red heels three times and go home.

George groans as he slides in the fetid mess of rotting food.

[*As* GEORGE] We don't want to use the fucking oxygen masks before we take off. Leave the doors open now for ventilation.

A soldier appears at the aircraft door.

[*As a* SOLDIER] Go back to hotel.

Driven back under armed escort.

Chaos. Lobby crammed. A mass of people.

Someone taps me on the shoulder. I turn and see. [*Directed out to the void*] Outside. Military bus after military bus arriving.

He taps me again.

[*As the* OFFICIAL] I am an official of the new Kuwaiti Government. I want to see all your passports.

And that's when the soldiers start dividing people up by nationality.

[*As the* OFFICIAL] American, British. Over there.

But we are preparing to leave.

[*As the* OFFICIAL] All other nationalities stand over there.

We were given permission to leave. We are to leave. Today.

[*As the* OFFICIAL] Two groups.

The soldiers are putting the passengers on the buses by nationalities—

These are not the orders.

[*As the* OFFICIAL] Our orders override all previous orders.

Why do you want to separate the nationalities?

Emma tries to conduct a head count for her lists. Soldiers push her away. Panic.

People jostling. Crying.

These people are in my care. At least keep the families together. Let the families stay together.

[*As the* OFFICIAL, *motioning*] You have no authority here. Go.

I stare this official down, this tyrant, with his, you, you, you, get on the buses.

[*To the camera*] Out there. In the world we once lived in. The British are doing nothing.

So I make up the big lie.

The British Embassy has informed me families must stay together. They view seriously any breach of this policy. The contempt and disgust of any official in dealing with British nationals will be brought to the immediate attention of Saddam Hussein himself.

[*As the* OFFICIAL] Families stay together.

[*To the camera*] I could do for them what I couldn't do for us, Amy.

I tell myself. They will never reach us once we are out of here. Amy is safe... that you are safe

My beautiful girl is safe.

[*To void space*] On a bus a woman is raped.

Crushed between the seat and a soldier with a gun.

We are taken out of the city in pitch black of night. On buses. Accompanied by fully armed soldiers in red armbands.

There's no moon. The Kuwaiti resistance are underground; they won't know this is a bus full of foreigners. A vehicle could be driven at top speed into the rear of the convoy, bombs strapped to the driver's chest. Heart beating. Perspiration dripping.

Finally we're out of that mess. Then... army camp. More soldiers.

Surround us. Stare at the women.

I hold Emma's hand. Make it look as if we are a couple. She's distressed.

[*As* EMMA] Captain. Take this list. Please. There are twelve missing people. They're on my list. They're males who are not here. But they should be. Here with us. They are on this passenger list. How can we find the missing men? I don't understand the code, the numbers next to their names.

Her soft hands press the paper into mine… like a love letter.

George has the dog.

Biggles wags his tail as a boot just misses his ribcage.

Dog sees it as a game and attacks one of their boots.

Dog unclean. Dog unclean.

The circle of soldiers tightens around us.

George takes the dog through his entire repertoire of tricks.

[*As* GEORGE] Beg! Walk on your hind legs. Roll over—and die for country.

The soldiers laugh.

They throw stained mattresses down. Stinking of urine. Sleep if you can. Rat-infested quarters. Pointed-shape droppings. Everywhere. Their randomness creates geometric patterns. A large bold rat sidles past. Biggles growls, snarls, lunges. A squeal and Biggles proudly drops the dead rat in his mouth at my feet.

I want to sleep next to you, Emma says. I don't feel safe.

But the Iraqis want males with males, females with females.

The women ask for the dog to go with them.

[*As a* SOLDIER] No. Dog stay here. Or dog…

The soldier makes a slitting motion with his finger across his throat.

The women are taken to another room I hear crying in the night. Morning. Passengers are separated from crew. Then Emma and the stewardesses are driven away. They vanish in a cloud of dust. All that is left is Emma's list caked with dirt. I hold Biggles. Soft little white body. Pink tongue hanging out. Looking at me with his big brown eyes. Full of trust. Keep me alive.

They put George, Justin and me on this hot clapped-out bus. Blindfold us.

*The* PILOT *shuts his eyes.*

We are driven for hours.

[*As the* SOLDIER] See, honoured guests! We bring you to the airport. You leave soon! But now we go past the airport hotel. You are not liking it there. We have something better for you.

Mind games.

[*As the* SOLDIER] Here, pilot, this is where you belong with your crew! Kuwait Air Force headquarters. Have something to eat. You are our guests. Watermelon and bread. Take off blindfolds!

> *The* PILOT *opens his eyes and physically recoils.*

There's shit everywhere. Shit in the washbasins. Shit all over upturned desks, chairs. Swarms of flies crawling over the shit. Gut churning.

This is where you sleep.

And carefully laid out in the mountains of shit are mattresses.

Clean all this shit up.

Wash it away with soap.

Soap smell. Sickening.

Soap smell still makes me sick.

All the washing-down of shit.

But at night…

> *The lights dim.*

… I see you. In your jamies. Perched on the end of my bed… Dad… Dad…

> *The* MAN *quietly sings an Arabic song of lament as he enters with a candle. He starts to chalk on the walls.*

Can you hear it, Amy? I am going into the labyrinth to fight the Minotaur. Stay with me, Amy.

Stay awake.

> *The* PILOT *picks up a torch. (The lights go down as he shines the torch.)*

Hold your torch. Shine the light on the Minotaur.

*The* PILOT *shines the torch over the walls.*

[*Whispering*] Where are we?

Babylon. See the portraits of Saddam everywhere, statues of Saddam, totally Saddam.

Everywhere.

Saddam meeting the honoured guests who cannot leave. The human shields.

See the small boy there eating broad beans.

[*As* SADDAM] Cute child. Good for photo.

Saddam patting him on the head.

[*As* SADDAM] Have you had your milk, Stewart?

Saddam beams.A benevolent father.

[*As* SADDAM] Now for the cameras. Smile!

See the terror in the child's eyes.

The hand patting the head.

Saddam putting his hand between the child's head and God.

The terror in the eyes.

The black box has no pictures of terror.

The black box tells only the story as recorded.

Your mother took a pair of scissors and cut me out of every family photo.

[*As the* PILOT'S WIFE] He can't be in the family snaps. He made my life a misery.

Now I am the blank space.

In a room in Baghdad, I was told to take off my name tag, my tie, and my epaulets. No more responsibilities.

You are no longer a pilot. Pilots are spies.

Standing by a curtain.

I nearly lost it. By that window…

Rinse, stack, wipe… rinse, stack, wipe…

I'd tried to be calm and philosophical up till then…

In uniform, you're a different person, it governs how you behave, what you believe is right and wrong. It's a responsibility and you take on that duty.

But when you're out of it… suddenly… and it's just you…

I didn't know who I was.

Now, I don't know who anybody else is.

Then all that mattered was the mateship.

George, Justin, Biggles and me hanging on together for dear life… [*takes off his pilot's shirt and rolls it up*] taken… Basra… southeast… a fertiliser factory… with a swimming pool… and the water's filthy… but we manage to get the filter going.

[*As* GEORGE] Aye! It's a weird fucking green colour, but hey fellas, this is our Club Med, let's have a dip in it anyway us three blokes on holiday at a fucking fertiliser plant! Three half naked men larking about playing catch with a wee dog in the middle of the fucking desert.

Upset the minders. No more outside! We're forced to eat and sleep inside.

[*As* GEORGE] Hang on a sec… fertiliser factory… fertilisers make explosives. Sodium nitrates. We could be fucking blown to bits in the blink of an eye. If I wanted to be blown up I could have stayed in fucking Belfast!

They move us to a petrochemical plant… vast complex. Made to sleep in the caustic chlorine unit. There's been a leak before we arrive… and immediately… we are the canaries. Strange, pungent, acrid smell. Burns the eyes and throat.

Our eyes sore, red and itching. Terrible headaches. Discharge. The little dog is dying [*cradles the shirt*].

We are bussed again to another location. An empty hospital… reeks of death.

The bus driver sits beside me. Smokes.

Cigarette? Please?

BUS DRIVER: [*teaching him how to ask in Arabic*] *Tismh le b jikarah?*

PILOT: *Gh… ji… cara?*

BUS DRIVER: *Jikarah.*

> *The* BUS DRIVER *sits beside the* PILOT, *carefully and covertly offering him a cigarette as he watches out for the guards. The* PILOT *takes several, which he hides in his shirt. The* BUS DRIVER *looks over his shoulder as if guards are nearby. The cigarettes/ matches exchanged.*

PILOT: Thank you.

BUS DRIVER: *Shukrun.*

PILOT: *Sho… shokrin…*

BUS DRIVER: *Shukrun.*

PILOT: *Shokun… shukrun!*

> *They laugh.*

BUS DRIVER: You are welcome to cigarettes… One-hundred welcomes. What is here?! My eyes play tricks?

PILOT: It would be too bad if this dog died.

BUS DRIVER: Here dog wild.

PILOT: Take the dog away from here. His name is Biggles.

BUS DRIVER: What is Biggle? Big?

PILOT: A daredevil pilot who fought for truth and justice.

BUS DRIVER: Never see like this. *Hatha eykhabil.* Nice animal. Very small like a doll.

PILOT: He is yours.

BUS DRIVER: What, how much?

PILOT: Do you have a radio?

BUS DRIVER: What, you take radio and I take Biggles?

PILOT: Ssshh. Quiet, yes.

*The* PILOT *hands him the dog (his rolled up shirt).*

BUS DRIVER: Okay… Yeah… yeah.

*He clicks his teeth as he carefully holds the towel.*

He's beautiful, very cute! [*In Arabic, as he gestures to pat the dog, see Appendix*] I like to give to my little daughter. But what my wife say if I give it to child?

[*As his* WIFE, *in Arabic, see Appendix*] From where you get it? Big problem if secret police see this. How you give our child this dog and keep? Everyone know it is not from here. Better leave on roadside.

*He hands the dog back.*

But if no-one take it, terrible if it die because it is hot and no water. Thirst is very bad, bring pain and make dog mad. But even leave it on road is danger… *Kattar*.

PILOT: [*an echo*] *Kattar*.

BUS DRIVER: The white LandCruiser car maybe come when I put dog there, the secret police get out. They say why do you touch dog?

I say it just ran out.

Why do you hold it?

Western guest give it to me.

Why do you touch it? Let it run on road and killed. It has something in it maybe, secret thing send beeps signals to enemy. Ah ha! You are helping enemy.

They take me to prison. Terrible stories people whisper. Sweat and blood on floor. Tie wires on your nipples… electric shock. Screams everywhere. Officers enjoy when take out your nail one by one then go home to dinner. They don't care. Push you down… on broken Pepsi bottle. Tie here… with cord then make you drink and drink. Hang you from hooks in the ceiling so arms rip apart. Throw you on the wall. Cages below… Attack dogs there… no food… starve; agitate with sticks, no need for execution when dogs free, like Roman Circus. Torture is time of fear. Fear in everyone's hearts. I want my family live in place with no torture. I want my wife happy… laughing... I am sorry for you people, not soldiers, same situation like me. I hate this bloody regime...

Look, I tell what I do. I come back… take dog late at night, take across border. I sell it. I get good money and Biggles gets better. I feel better… one less suffering in the time of fear… Peace be upon you. *Ma'ah ssalamah.*

> The PILOT *and* BUS DRIVER *shake hands.*

> *The* BUS DRIVER *exits.*

PILOT: Biggles saved and I am weeping, in the bus driver's jacket, a radio.

The sound of Bow bells. The sound of hope.

[*British accent*] Wherever you are. However you listen. This is the BBC World Service. Today we start Gulf Link. Taped messages for those held in Iraq.

I'm not ready for this.

Your little voice on the radio.

[*As* AMY] Dad, this is Amy. I miss you. I want you home for Christmas. I love you.

It's hard. It screws me up. Hearing your voice…

> *He tries to gather his composure.*

*SCENE THREE*

*The lights become brighter.*

PILOT: [*almost bewildered*] What is the last terror? It comes by stealth.

It is unseen.

I watch.

The dust storm behind him.

The farmer's boy.

A small dot.

The wind gathers.

[*As* FARMER'S SON] I forgot, mister. Dad said… she and her fuck monkey wants to meet youse.

His voice lost.

Who?

[*As the* FARMER'S SON] She's your daughter.

What?

[*As the* FARMER'S SON] Dunno, mister. Someone rang my dad… Dad reckons all Muzzies wear bombs around their waist and are crazy. He don't want no trouble.

Come back here.

[*As the* FARMER'S SON] Crazy mothafuckas… he reckons. [*In a singsong voice*] Crazy mothafuckas… crazy motha… How much money you got?

Little bastard is blackmailing me. Get lost! Go on, clear off, you little prick.

I pay the farmer. All my mail sent to him under his name. Pay him big money. But if there's trouble will he turn informer?

[*To the camera*] Now you are making trouble for me, Amy. This is a big problem.

Yes, this man you've met, this Hassan, could be a good bloke.

Or it could be a set-up.

Why do you do this?

Why?

Do you see how blood and terror rules us all?

[*To void space*] Nothing is ever the same after a war.

When I returned from Iraq I signed a document of silence, acknowledging the power of the state to keep its secrets.

But there was one thing I denied them.

What intelligence want from me is Emma's list.

Emma had standards. Truth was one of them. Being liked another. Always helpful. They questioned her. They questioned all of us. Do the right thing for national security. I saw her briefly.

Don't worry, she says. I understand there was nothing you could do. No hard feelings. People come and go in life but families stay together... unity. Pulling together. Intelligence want that list.

She tells them she gave it to me. I tell them it was taken from me.

The Iraqi soldiers searched me. Kicked me as I lay in the dust. Their hands searched my pockets, and then they stuffed my mouth full of sand. Take my list.

A list is not mysterious, it's scientific, Amy. Every passenger on flight 149 passes through the checkpoint at Heathrow. The employee that day, now works in the  labyrinthine corridors of the Defence Ministry. BA claims the list of passengers has long gone missing. No records have been kept. But all the names are on my list. The shadowy secrets of state-sponsored terrorism. You could think this was all inside my head. Look at the facts.

[*As* GEORGE] No-one knows what we saw. We have to fucking promise not to betray each other. Keep the faith, comrade. Strength through unity.

But then he disappeared. No trace. Went on a road trip and never came home.

Justin wrote to me once. [*As* JUSTIN] Don't call. Don't contact me. Too dangerous.

Then nothing. We were all tied together, and now the mateship is broken.

This black box records how I lose control of the plane. Descent at a sharp angle. Where is Utopia, the place I was brought up to believe in? The good society.

Full throttle, manual crosschecks, battery check… cross-feed valves… can feel the plane falling…

Don't know where the sky or ground is… no visibility… rolling… pressure leaking away… tiny grains of sand going through the turbines will blow the engine apart.

Saddam lets the French go.

The Germans go.

Then the Americans are freed because Muhammad Ali comes to bring them home.

Everyone can go but the British… and their employees. Then a miracle.

Miracles happen.

Thatcher gets kicked out as Prime Minister! Thrown out by her own party.

So Saddam had this overwhelming feeling of euphoria.

*Let them all go!*

They fly us out on Iraqi Airways.

There is a great cheer and clapping as the plane is airborne.

They are celebrating life.

As I look down I see death.

Somewhere in the sand drifts. My plane is on a runway. I've abandoned her. Millions of pounds of equipment.

Who am I?

   *The* MAN *enters behind the* PILOT.

A passenger.

On an Iraqi Airways jumbo manned by Iraqi pilots.

That plane flies into Gatwick.

[*To the camera*] After 9/11, the British would have blown that plane up. Too unsafe… terrorists could be flying it. We would have died. Instead we die a slow death.

[*To void space*] Death by a thousand cuts.

A month later. The Gulf War. The Coalition of the Willing comes to liberate Kuwait. The Americans are on a crusade from God.

Now my plane, the plane I was responsible for, is destroyed. By fleeing Iraqis?

My plane is destroyed by a USA fighter plane. Friendly fire.

Torn apart. All that's left of BA 149… black wreckage on the tarmac.

Twisted tail. Wheels torn away. A carcass. The carnage begins.

I see it on the TV.

The video games of war.

The unidentified.

The faceless ones.

Night after night.

The dead and the dying.

What if I see his face on the screen?

More vivid and real than in my dreams.

What if I hear his voice?

This Arab, this bus driver who saved Biggles.

This man who made me feel that struggle was shared.

> *As the* PILOT *speaks, the* BUS DRIVER *speaks in Arabic—living the story.*

BUS DRIVER: I need cigarette. *Areed jigarah.*

PILOT: [*an echo, in Arabic*] *Areed jigarah.*

BUS DRIVER: *Inteeni jigarah.*

PILOT: [*in English*] Give me cigarette.

> *The* PILOT *speaks the following in English, the* BUS DRIVER *in Arabic, see Appendix.*

BUS DRIVER & PILOT: [*simultaneously*] Burning hot, everyone fleeing.

Workers in bus, mothers, children. Raining from the sky, a thousand bombs. No rifles. No guns. No cover. Shells bursting above. Trapped.

Tie a white shirt from the bus window.

We are not enemies, America.

Mile after mile, twisted metal cars, taxis, smouldering heaps of lorries. No way back or forward on highway of death. Desperate. Cut us like ribbons. Bombs shrieking above us. Don't stop. Blast us all away.

But still Bush call on us. We help you. Rise up against Saddam. Don't stop now.

I go to town square. Handkerchief on all faces. We fear to show faces.

Saddam's soldiers there… they shoot at us. Wound me. Saddam's helicopters dump chemicals. I lie down my face to the ground. I cannot breathe, I see tears. Where are the Americans? Why do they do so little?

My body is cold.

Saddam soldiers think I am dead.

I flee with my family in morning.

My wife sick. I carry my child.

My wife looks back as we walk, weeps to see dust and ashes and columns of smoke from great shrine.

You talk of your child. What about my child?

My child starves. No milk.

My wife goes to the River Tigris. Hidden by the grasses of the river is hundreds-years-old shrine to St George. Muslims and Christians for generations believe this a holy shrine.

She prays for help there.

She wraps herself in her burqa and goes early morning when secret police do not see her.

They forbid the women to come there.

The place in the mud.

Kneel on the slippery stones.

Hand on the stones worn away by the breath of prayers.

Washed green with the moss of tears.

The Defence Ministry with its torture chambers is on the opposite bank of the river.

Its windows stare down like a thousand black eyes on her.

She must hurry.

She lights a candle. Places candle on a small piece of bark. Hands shake as she pushes it into the water. Watches it float away.

St George. Help me, St George. Will my child eat again? Please to give her food. If the candle does not blow out, make my wish come true…

Candle blows out.

My child dies.

BUS DRIVER: [*in Arabic*] *Binty il sighra matet.*

PILOT: [*an echo*] *Binty il sighra matet.*

BUS DRIVER: [*in English*] My child dies. My child dies.

>    *The* BUS DRIVER *turns away, his back to the* PILOT. *Exits.*

PILOT: [*an echo*] *My child dies.*

They will find you, Amy. They will hunt you down.

Sitting here, waiting for the assassins.

>    *The lights flicker.*

>    *The* PILOT *quietly gets up. He listens.*

What game are they playing now?

Outside.

Their preferred method of dispatchment is always outside. No DNA on the premises. No physical evidence. Get him outside, they'll be saying, get him out! He'll check the fuse boxes.

Or is it just a faulty light bulb?

Test the other lights.

Risky.

Don't stand near the window.

Shards of broken glass. He fell, they'll say. Gashed an artery.

The *shamal*… the *simoom*… the sandstorms.

Terror contaminates.

Terror infects your mind.

No clear thoughts, just whirling spirals of doubt. Sickening. Choking.

If they want to kill me in cold blood, they'll have to smoke me out.

  *Almost casually as he puts his shirt back on and buttons it up.*

If I run now… cigarette can act as a fuse.

Empty the petrol can under the car. Smoke the cigarette. Two puffs. Drop cigarette under car. Run like hell. Cigarette slow burn, matches light in petrol.

Explosion.

*Bang!*

That'll attract the attention of the farmer. The assassins will melt away. If I wait… one will come inside and one will watch outside.

If I kill the one who comes inside I get his gun.

I need a knife or an axe.

I saw Saddam swing.

I'd like to see all of them swing.

The right-wing fundamentalists of the West

Who drove us all to war.

[*Whispering*] They're inside.

Stealth.

Under the cover of darkness.

No mercy.

Control. Persecute.

Crush. Eradicate.

He's a dog. String him up on the wire fence.

A fifty-year-old male was found. Hanging from a tree. Tongue stuck out. Blue. Bright blue. For the sake of the family no further enquiry. Case closed. No suspicious circumstances. Memory obliterated.

The assassins have gathered to watch the pilot fall from the sky like burning wreckage.

*Pause.*

[*To the camera*] How can you fight the undefined enemy?

Stream the names on Emma's list. I'll stream the names of the passengers on flight BA 149. Pin the list to the uniform.

*The* PILOT, *for the first time, puts on his jacket.*

Zoom in.

*The* PILOT *turns the chair to face the camera. Sits. He lights the match. Holds it close to his jacket until the flame blows out.*

This is the list of names of the twelve men, the agents, the ex-SAS, the military who were on that plane.

Don't be afraid.

I won't let them hurt you.

Even though I could never be a father to you.

I failed.

I regret that most.

Amy love.

I will never see you again.

It's over.

I love you… and if this Hassan… loves you…

*The* PILOT *reaches out touches the camera, then switches it off.*

The pilot is finished.

But so are they.

It is out there.

PILOT *scatters the matches over the floor and tosses away the matchbox.*

And the Arab is still beside me. Looking at me. Laughing with me.

*Pause.*

The farmer... he pays them to come here with their sniper rifles and shotguns to hunt wild dogs. Bullets this long. They wait till dusk when the animals want to drink. Still so hot the men just wear singlets and shorts... after the kill they flay and hang the skins on the barbed wire.

The knot in the guts.

> *The* PILOT *places his pilot's cap on his head. For the first time in the play he is dressed in full Pilot's uniform. Pause.* PILOT *steps out of the front of the box transgressing its boundaries.*
>
> *Sound effects of Iraqi music and video footage of a collage of images: the massacre by the U.S. airforce of retreating soldiers and civilians from Kuwait, 'the highway of death', the 1991 Iraqi uprising against the rule of Saddam Hussein and his brutal retaliation with his Republican Guard against the civilians at Karbala. The images spill over* PILOT *and box, and are timed against his last words.*

The wild dog is dangerous.

> *Pause.*

It doesn't obey.

> *Pause.*

Just shoot it in the head.

> *Pause.*

*Kattar.*

> *Pause.*

Out in the dust.

> *Pause.*

Out in the dust.

> *Blackout.*

## THE END

*First Interrogator scene*

'If the matchbox in this position, I am King here…' (Page 17)

Formal Arabic

اذا كانت عُلبة الكبريت بهذا الوضع أنا سأكون الملك

Informal Iraqi

اذا صـارت علبة الكبريت بهذا الوضع، اني راح اكون الملك


'If you flip it right way… you are the guest…' (Page 17)

Formal Arabic

اذا انتَ رميتها بوضع صحيح ، انت ستكون الضيف

Informal Iraqi

اذا انته شمرتها بوضع صحيح ، انته الضيف


'Who were these people…?' (Page 18)

Formal Arabic

مَن هؤلاء الناس؟

Informal Iraqi

منو هذوله الناس؟

'What is your rank in the army?' (Page 18)

Formal Arabic

مَاهي رتبتك العسكريّه؟

Informal Iraqi

شنو رتبتك العسكريّه؟

*Take a look at these photos.* (Page 19)

Formal Arabic

انظر الى هذه الصور!

Informal Iraqi

شوف هاي الصور

'What is being unloaded?' (Page 19)

Formal Arabic

ما الذي يتم تحميله؟

Informal Iraqi

اشجاي يحمّلون؟

'What are they?' (Page 19)

Formal Arabic

ماهي؟

Informal Iraqi

شنو هنه؟

'Tracking devices.' (Page 20)

Formal Arabic

أجهزةُ تعقب.

Informal Iraqi

أجهزة مال تعقب.

'I can take you there and you can have a look.' (Page 20)

Formal Arabic

أستطيع أن آخذك الى هناك وتنظر بنفسك.

Informal Iraqi

أكدر اخذك لهناك وتشوف ابنفسك.

'What is your favourite film?… Have you seen…?' (Page 20)

Formal Arabic

ماهو فلمكِ المفضّل؟..... هل شاهدت....؟

Informal Iraqi

شنو الفلم المفضّل الك؟...هم شايف....؟

'Two years.' (Page 20)

Formal Arabic

سنتان

Informal Iraqi

سنتين

*Second Interrogator scene*

'Blonde piggytails, blue eyes.' (Page 23)

Formal Arabic

ذيل أشقر كذيل صغير الخنزير. عينان زرقاوتان

Informal Iraqi

ذيا اشكر مثل ذيل الخنزير الزغير. اعيون زركه

'When streets are filled with the dead…' (Page 24)

Formal Arabic

عندما تملأ الشوارع بالموتى......

Informal Iraqi

لمن تنملي الشوارع بالموته......

*Bus driver scene*

'Why do you hold it?' (Page 33)

Formal Arabic

لمَ تحمله؟

Informal Iraqi

ليش شايله؟

'Why do you touch it? Let it run on road and killed.' (Page 33)

Formal Arabic

لمَ تلمسه؟ دعهُ يهرب على الطريق ويقتل.

Informal Iraqi

ليش اتلزمه؟ عوفه ينهزم على الطريق وينكتل.

*Arabic words from the Bus Driver to the Pilot about the dog*
(Page 33)

Informal Iraqi

لك هذا الجلب كلش حلو، ايخبّل!!!!

Lak Hatha Echaleb Kuolesh heloo Eykhabil.

This dog is very beautiful, cute!

\*

*Arabic words the Bus Driver imagines his wife saying about
the dog* (Page 33)

Informal Iraqi

امّين جبت هذا يامعزّه؟

يمعود هذا ايسويّلنه مشكله اذا الأمن شافوه.

Immean jibit Hatha Yamazzah?
Yamauwad Iysaweelnah Mushkelah Itha alaman shafoh.

From where did you get this you idiot? It would create a big problem
for us if the secret police see it.

\*

'Terrible stories people whisper. Sweat and blood on floor.' (Page 33)

## Formal Arabic

قصص رهيبه يتداولها الناس بهمس. الدماء والعَرَق على الارض.

## Informal Iraqi

سوالف رهيبه الناس تحجيها ابيناتهم ابهمس. الدمايات والعرك على الكاع

'Torture is time of fear. Fear in everyone's hearts.' (Page 33)

## Formal Arabic

التعذيب هو مايخيف. الخوف في قلوب الجميع.

## Informal Iraqi

التعذيب هو الي يخوّف. الخوف بكلوب الكل.

*Bus driver's monologue spoken with the Pilot. Broken into sections written in informal street parlance and the formal (literal to script) form*

**From** 'Burning hot' … **To** 'We are not enemies, America.'
(Pages 38–39)

### Informal Iraqi

اشتعلت بينا شعل، الكل تنهزم . عمال بالشّاحنات، أمّهات، أطفال. السما تمطر الاف القنابل. ماكو بنادق ولا
رشاشات ولاملجأ. القذايف تتفجر فوكانا، ورّطه. طلع وصله بيضه من شباج الباص، احنه مو أعداء امريكا

### Formal Arabic

أحترقت الدنيا، الكل ينهزم. عمال بالشاحنات، أمّهات، أطفال. السّماء تمطر الاف القنابل. لابنادق لدينا، لأسلـ
ولاملجأ. القذائف تتفجر فوق رؤوسنا، انها مصيده. أخرج راية بيضاء من شباك الحافلة. نحن لسنا بأعداءكـ
أمريكا.

\*

**From** 'Mile after mile' … **To** 'Blast us all away.'
(Page 39)

### Informal Iraqi

ميل بعد ميل، سيارات متحطمه، تاكسيات، أكوام متفحمه من اللوريات. ماكو روحه ولا رجعه على طريق الموت
الرئيسي. الجزع يلقنه ومتكطعين مثل الشرايط. القنابل تصرخ فوكانا، ماتوكف اتكطعنه تكطيع.

### Formal Arabic

ميل بعد آخر، سيارات محطمة، سيارت أجره، اكوامٌ متفحمة من الشاحنات. ليس هناك ذهاب أو اياب على طريق
الموت السريع. الجزع يلفنا، نتقطعُ مثل الاشرطه. القنابلُ تصرخُ فوق رؤوسنا بلا توقف، تَمزّقنا اربا.

\*

### From 'But still Bush' … To 'Why do they do so little?'
(Page 39)

### Informal Iraqi

لكن بوش بعده ايخاطبنا " راح انساعدكم، انتفضوا على صدام، لاتوكفون. "

روح للولايه، انغطي اوجوهنه بالغتر، خاف نكشف أوجوهنه. جماعة صدام هناك، يرمون علينه. اني انجرح. طيارات الهليكوبتر مال صدام تضرب علينه كيمياوي. انبطح أوّوجهي على الكاع، ماأكدر اتنفس، بس احس بالدموع. وين الامريكان؟؟ ليش كلشي مديسوون؟؟

### Formal Arabic

لكن بوش ظلّ يدعونا، " سوف نساعكم، انتفظوا على صدام، لاتقفوا."

وجّه لمركز المدينه. نغطي وجوهنا بالكوفيات كي لاننكشف. جنذُ صدام المتمركزين هناك يطلقون النار علينا، انا أجرح. طائرات الهليكوبتر لحرس صدام ترمينا بالاسلحة الكيمياوية. انبطح ووجهي على الارض. احسُّ بالدموع تجري، لااستطيع ان اتنفس. اين الامريكان؟ لمَ لمْ يقوموا بأيِّ شيْ؟

\*

### From 'My body is cold.' … To 'smoke from great shrine.'
(Page 39)

### Informal Iraqi

جسمي يبرد، جنود صدام عبّالهم اني ميت. أنهزم اني وعاتلتي الصّبح. زوجتي مريضه وطفلتي تصرخ. زوجتي تباوع وراها وهيّه تمشي. تبجي ابحرگه لمّا أتشوف الغبار والدخان طالع من المرقد.

### Formal Arabic

برد جسمي، جند صدام يعتقدون بانّيّ ميت. أغادر وعائلتي صباحا". زوحتي مريضة وطفلتي تصرخ. زوجتي تنظرورائها وهي تمشي. تبكي بحرقة عندما ترى الغبار وأعمدة الدخان تتصاعد من المرقد.

\*

**From** 'You talk of your child.' … **To** 'She prays for help there.' (Page 39)

## Informal Iraqi

انته تحجي عن طفلتك،!! زين وطفلتي؟ طفلتي جاي اتموت من الجوع، ماعدهه حليب.

زوجتي اتروح النهر دجله. هناك بين الحشيش أكو مرقد مال خضر الياس صاره مئات السنين، مسلمين أومسيحين يعتقدون ويؤمنون بيه. زوجتي اتصلي اهناك.

## Formal Arabic

تتحدث عن طفلتك!! وماذا عن طفلتي؟ طفلتي تتضور جوعا، ليس لديها حليب يكفي.

زوجتي تذهب الى نهر دجلة. هناك بين الحشائش يقعُ مرقدٌ قديم منذ مئات السنين لخضرالياس. عبر اجيال مسلمين ومسيحين يؤمنون به. زوجتي تصلي هناك.

\*

**From** 'She wraps herself' … **To** 'like a thousand black eyes on her.' (Pages 39–40)

## Informal Iraqi

تلف نفسهه بالعبايه وتروح الصبح غبشه حتى الأمن مايشوفوهه، لانه منعوا كل الناس من الرّوحه لهناك. المك بين الطين والحجار. تركع، اتشوف طبع الايدين على الصخور تركتها آثار المصلين وأنفاسهم. تغسل الصخور بالدمع. وزارة الدفاع على الضفة الثانية من النهر، هيه وغرف التعذيب اللي بيهه. اشبابيجها كأنه عيون سود اتخنزر عليهه.

## Formal Arabic

تلف نفسها بعبائتها. تذهب الفجر كي لا يراها رجال الأمن السريّ، فقد منعوا كل النساء من الذهاب الى هناك تركع، ترى طبع الايدي على الصخور تركتها آثار المصلين وأنفاسهم. تغسلُ الصّخور بالدّمع. وزراة الدفاع عا الضّفة المقابلة بغرف التعذيب العديدة تقبع هناك. كأن شبابيكها عيون سوداء تحدق فيها بخزر

\*

### From 'She must hurry' … To 'My child dies.'
(Page 40)

### Informal Iraqi

لازم تسرع. تشعل شمعه، أتحطه على قطعه من الخشب. ايديه ترجف أوهيّه اتحطها على المي، اتراقبيه أوهيّه اطوف. يالخضر... ساعدني يالخضر، هم طفلتي راح اتعيش؟ ابجاهك ارزقها يالخضر. اذا الشمعه ما انطفت، نذري يتحقق. الشمعه تنطفي..... أوطفلتي اتموت.

### Formal Arabic

جب ان تسرع. تُشعلُ شمعة، تضعُها على قطعةٍ من الخشب، يدها ترتجف وهي تضعها على سطح الماء، تُراقبها هي تطوف. ايَها الخضر، ساعدني ايّا الخضر. هل ستعيش طفلتي وتأكل؟ ارزقها بجاهك. اذا لم تنطفيء الشَمعة سوف يتحقق نذري. الشَمعة تنطفيْ .... وطفلتي تموت.

\*

### *Words of the Arabic song MAN sings*
(Page 10)

### Lyrics in Iraqi

مالي صحت يمّه احّا جا وين اهلنه ؟

جا وين

جا وين اهلنه؟

Oh, what's wrong with me?
I say where is my family?
Where is
Where is my family?